The Park

Books by John Freeman

The Park

JOHN FREEMAN

COPPER CANYON PRESS

PORT TOWNSEND, WASHINGTON

Cover art: *Empty Chairs Amidst Trees at Park*
by Alexandre Blondeau / EyeEm / Getty Images

Copper Canyon Press is in residence at Fort Worden State Park
in Port Townsend, Washington, under the auspices of Centrum.
Centrum is a gathering place for artists and creative thinkers
from around the world, students of all ages and backgrounds,
and audiences seeking extraordinary cultural enrichment.

LIBRARY OF CONGRESS CATALOGING-IN-PUBLICATION DATA
Names: Freeman, John, 1974– author.
Title: The park / John Freeman.
Description: Port Townsend, Washington : Copper Canyon Press, [2020] |
Identifiers: LCCN 2019043064 | ISBN 9781556595950 (trade paperback)
Subjects: LCGFT: Poetry.
Classification: LCC PS3606.R445465 P37 2020 | DDC 811/.6—dc23
LC record available at https://lccn.loc.gov/2019043064

98765432 FIRST PRINTING

COPPER CANYON PRESS
Post Office Box 271
Port Townsend, Washington 98368
www.coppercanyonpress.org

This book is for Teri Boyd and Aleksandar Hemon,
friends, groundskeepers, guides

City parks are not abstractions, or automatic repositories of virtue or uplift, any more than sidewalks are abstractions. They mean nothing divorced from their practical, tangible uses, and hence they mean nothing divorced from the tangible effects on them—for good or for ill—of the city districts and uses touching them.

Jane Jacobs, *The Death and Life of Great American Cities*

*How do we come to be here next to each other
in the night
Where are the stars that show us to our love
inevitable*

June Jordan, "Poem for My Love"

Contents

The Park

The Sacrifice

The difference
between animals and us
the main one is
they don't need to know
it's a park. The coyote
lopes through
just the same
looking for food. We
stop, in mourning,
sensing everything
we've lost. We call
that ceremony
a park.

Modern Gods

Backlit by the glow
from a small passageway,
he kneels into the fog
of yellow light,
head kissing the carpet.
I step around him,
respecting his privacy, when
the mat becomes not prayer
rug but builder's tool,
a black piece of tarmac laid down
before the bank so he could
peer close, fix the dead
motion sensor so that people
with money could
be seen, all doors opening
for them.

Unfinished

She never saw it completed,
did not glimpse the many
varieties of tortoises
that lounged in a pond
near the north gate, never
peered into its vast fish pool,
never lowered her voice upon
stepping into the medal
room, her son's decoration
shimmering in its ambition.
She, being a woman, had to
move in while the making was
still being made, 1625,
interiors sawdust and silk. Mornings padding
across cold marble floors past footmen
clicking heels together, the arc
of her life there for all to see
in twenty-four Rubenses—girlhood,
motherhood, widowhood.
How they resented her,
the French, but needed her
money. She would have to
commission her own story. She
just needed more time, but time
knows when it is being chased.
The cardinals and ministers did not
even hide the whetstone.
They would eat
her. Sailing to the Spanish
Netherlands, banished
to Belgium, did she know
she'd never see her beloved park again? Or did
it occur to her, finally, she could never
replace time with time? Even a third

of a century building was not enough
to return her childhood
for a moment. So she gave
the park to her son, the second
son, in the full throes
of his dukedom, an expert in
acquisition. He'd never
understand the only things
that matter are irreplaceable. Then the palace began
to tumble through the ages,
each exchange erasing what
it was meant to replace, developers
nibbling at its margins, Napoleon
ripping up her fountain, urban
planners stuffing its walks
with statuaries, a hundred
thousand kisses exchanged
in its shadows every
spring. Even the
Nazis in 1940 passed through
and the Luftwaffe said, this will do.

It's sleeting today, winter, the park
glistens in its blanket of cold. By
noon the snow will be gone,
an easy embrace to refuse.

Visitors

I've counted six sides
up Vaugirard, across Guynemer
a short bit on d'Assas,
the long stretch up
rue de Auguste-Comte
then over blvd Saint-Michel
down the hill of rue de Médicis past
Le Rostand and the Sénat
where the guards stand
with self-conscious weaponry.
One side features blown-up
photographs of polar bears
on ice, like all animals captured
in the moment of being
animals, bewildered annoyed
saddened, one might think,
by our need to record what is
obvious: they're at home.
What our looking has done
to them—elegies to themselves.

In the park this violet
hour of dawn, walkers
runners in the shadows
of trees men with backpacks and
darting eyes look out sideways
with similar glances,
don't want to be seen,
need to be seen, so we feel
ourselves feeling their predicament,
two hours here while the shadows
remain. The men move on.

On the other side of Paris
an exhibit depicts their home
which is nowhere. By nine
the Norwegian walking club gathers.
Smart cross-country poles
bulging retirement portfolios,
they'll be gone across the city
no exhibit, a man or two,
dirty enough to create the kinds
of shadows that make it easy not to see him.

The Ex-Basketball Players

The ex-basketball players
want to tell me what
it was like playing youth
tournaments during
the war how hilariously and
inappropriately they were dressed
this guy was shot they say
pointing to their point guard
now a conductor
a detail that produces roars
he has scars
for a moment I think he's
going to lift his shirt the quietest
and drollest of the group
instead he talks of an all-night drive back
to Sarajevo in 1995 and how
bandaged and bleeding
into his uniform he told the bus driver
I can't go back
got out with three friends in
Slovenia four a.m.
we took some sleep he says
in the park and phoned a friend of
a friend who asked how we were
three teenagers in a park at dawn
I had this much money in my pocket
we said fine we are okay but two days
later we weren't we had just twenty
euros our agent stalling she
didn't want us showing up smelly in
Italy so the friend of a friend took
us in for a few days it was nice showers
hot food no shelling but by day three
claps hands that's it boys so it's time

for our agent to come through and miraculously
she does we're on a train
across Europe as if our homes aren't on
fire sitting with travelers reading
newspapers as if our sisters aren't
being shot and for months the agent
she shopped us around Europe
taking us to tournaments tryouts
maybe our price was too high
the four of us it was fucking hysterical
no one wants a refugee on their team
we were like four monkeys on a rope
That's when they all double over in
laughter and form a circle and hug
and someone changes the subject

Separation

Two birds cross the mossed sky, reflected in the Naviglio
Pavese at dawn. Standing on the bridge, looking down, I know

if I peer up to find them the air will be muddy and dull, they
will simply be a set of wings diagonaling a day's

beginning, as how in some kinds of love,
beauty lies in the separation.

Open All Night

The park beneath the park
is open all night,
people sprawl
across benches,
this way and
that, one man sits straight up
as if in a pew, eyes
closed, bags at his
feet, rocking to
the rhythm of the park
beneath the park.

You can stroll here,
take your coffee,
you may even on occasion
feel the whisper of a breeze
as we rush into the Mabillon
station, the slatted windows
of this park on wheels
letting you know there is
a world outside, a place
above where

on graveled quadrants
we are not alone, where
a sound beneath every
sound says, we are not alone,
and you can feel it,
like a humming in the blood, how
when there is no hawk falling like
a blade, no wolf loping
into view, no marmot
nosing the cracks in what
we made of its pavement

we are lonely and ashamed.
We are too much ourselves,

and we sit, one to a bench,
sometimes if the stink is too
much, one man to a whole
carriage, riding in the park
beneath the park, erasing the dark
hours in the white electric light.

Almost Snowing

The sky is white
a light shone
behind a pillow

I lift the window
and stick out
my head a blind

angel tells me
to sniff the air
tastes of glass
wet building ice
remember this
she says she
always does
as if there's
room inside me
for everything

Seeing Things

Now the trees rush, crackle
in the dark. I sleep like a
sailor on night watch. I was told,
look in the shadows for figures
that
        freeze. I can see straight
through the park. There
are the camps. There beds.
There, a man, washing his foot
in rainwater. You do not
need to be a hawk to
see here. No one talks
of this, how winter doesn't just
strip bare, it allows us to see
what's always been there.

The Death Givers

Almost all statuaries were killers;
if on horseback, add ten thousand
to the toll. And sword-bearers?
Notch another zero. We think
we worship life, but we have
made a botch of this, encircling
ponds and trees with the smelt
of disused weapons, planting flowers
around the ankles of killers,
even the birds know not to use them
as lighthouses. Death
is our archangel, our leaders
bronze themselves in advance—
even a dog can't trot through the palace
halls these days without looking over
its shoulder.

Translation in Paris

There are no editors in the café
called Les Éditeurs. There's not
a single novelist in the Saint-
Germain store gilded by novels.
There are no beasts of the chase
paddocked in the park, but that's what

the West Germanic word—*parruk*—meant.

It took the overrunning of London
by its immigrant population in the 1680s
to turn the word into the spot we'd
park humans, so they could stumble
around in bewilderment at how time
is translation, change is nature's rime.

The City Without

All publics have their useless intensities—
it's what makes them public. A park's
purpose is to temper the machine
in us. A city without parks snarls all day
heaving and bragging, believes the carols
of its admirers, while most people living
in it spend their day canyoning through
waterfalls of traffic, scaling monuments,
heads down, pilgrims who find themselves
too far upriver to turn back from where they come.

In a Bucharest Journal

I'm writing you with the part of me that
can remember the view
of Cișmigiu, so misty at dawn.
That dog is still down there yowling in
the cold. Write me when the books
arrive. On page 36 I have left
something for you—I hope
it is enough. Read it, imagine
me listening without trying.
Did you see the tiny girl
at the factory
last night, eating cake?

To think she could
have been ours.

Winter Diary

I walk through the park
toward Montparnasse
to meet Livia for
a drink. It's raining at last,
gray and slow, as it should at
every funeral. At the park's
exit a white dog
sniffs the air. The day
shuts down, a bulk-
head heaved
shut, only there's no
clatter, just a new
density to the rain falling
without light, against
itself into darkness,
as if for once air and color
are the same thing,
and one part of the world's
unity has been restored.

The Politician

Night conspires to hide his gloom,
this falcon born of air and fire,
wicked plume. Who could desire to sit
in such a chair, beneath gothic spire,
giving midnight scare? Yet here
he is in the Sénat this moonlit
night, clouds scudding her bone-white
sight, counting rats and fowl,
pinstriped, proud, knowing these
once-private chambers are locked
again from the filthy crowd.

January

I cooked pasta
with chilies last
night and my
fingers still
burn. It's how the mind
feels these days,
you say, upon
arrival, and we
sit with this. I
am so angry
I cannot
touch you.

Reprieve

Stepping out into a slate-gray
morning, the smell of rain,
Robespierre said, *not today,*
before returning to a fugitive bed.
Thirty death sentences can wait
for one more. Or was killing
like an arrow of sunlight on a cold
day. As in, once you walk from
the cold into the heat, you do not
want to leave that tiny plenitude.

II

Signs

Chestnut buds green the trees. How
time operates on the mind, winding
it like a clock, when we believe
we're the ones tuning it.

On Love

I leave the spread of your hair and walk
into the park, sit in the hollow of night's
carcass. Others are here, lovers stranded
by love. Islands beneath a cerulean sky.

They stare into the trees, not looking, not
searching, but holding the small part
of themselves they do not give, in order to
give, cupping it, like tiny blue flames.

Birds

On the edge of Jardin du Luxembourg nightjars fret
the dark, shrikes pace the grounds, that fierce khanjar
between the eyes. This week chiffchaff clocked in,
flitting branch to branch on stockinged legs, plumage
pale as an emerald soaked in water. Whoever named
them "common" suffers an ordinary mind. Wrens
arrived, too, churring and scolding, singing about love.
Somewhere a peregrine sits above it all in silence,
targeting, eyes ringed in yellow. Valkyrie of dominion.
How often to prey one must be silent and alone.
Whoever named a pistol grip a "bird's head" was
looking at something without wonder, something dead.

Weight

What if each time
you caused pain
a small round stone
were put in your pocket
pebbles for inducing
self-doubt
osmium for death.
When you heard
someone approach
their pockets noisy
you'd know,
just as dogs do,
to keep distance.
Some men
would pull wagons
behind them,
their pants disfigured.
They'd be shamed
from sidewalks
delayed at customs,
they could never
lie flat on beds.
They'd have
to stand feeling
the weight of
what they'd done.

Spring

We stroll home in soft May sunlight
our grief so small it does not require
solitude or silence. One morning, smelling of honeysuckle
and mint, you return from the market
prepare a tuna salad, breaking up the meat with your hands
shake the last of the oil from the jar, a new kind of silence
created by your movement in the kitchen, one that takes
the sounds I sat with at this table, by the blue window
reminding me all of them had been the sound of your absence.

Teacher

We knew she'd loved
been loved by how she
taught Shakespeare,
the anguish of regret
staining her voice
when Henry turns his
back on Falstaff, denies
a love untidy. She saw
in us these untidinesses,
loved us for them.
That's not too strong a
word, is it, for how a teacher
tends the statuaries she
places in students' minds?
Thick is the green
there with longing and
fury, little pebbled
by regret or patience. What
tenderness it takes to
plant, such a lot
of raking, weeding, a
respect for the ground
itself, and yet she
showed us a love that
didn't ravage equally
was not love,
it could make you weep
before a room of teenagers,
caged in self-mockery. She dared
us to feel, even for her. How old
she seemed, scarves in
springtime, pilgrimages to
Ravello in summer, eyes misty
every fall at the spectacle of

our unzippering before her
beloved bard, etched onto
our skins now
a passionate kiss.

Ordering a Café in Paris

The true divas
of this city are
its waiters. There
he goes, platter
raised, spinning
away from me
again, all eyes
follow him
as he slips between
tables like a
dancer around
unworthy partners,
the swivel-hipped
youth of the
ugly-handsome
school. Just one
look, a glance!
We are his rapt
audience.
A circuit complete,
now he appears
to be contemplating
the rain. He's
sensitive, too. I wait,
memorizing my lines,
praying I will
not stumble
the moment
he's suddenly
standing over me,
beauty the barrier
to beauty, asking
me what it is
that I want.

Somewhere You Are Sleeping

and the lights are out, the lights of your eyes, the shine in your hair, fanned
    across the pillow,
it breathes at night   did you know this?
    The room is dark,
and here in Paris the city wakes, fitful and furious, everyone clutching
    their private
agonies on the metro. I am ordering coffee and a croissant and I hear you mimicking my
    accent,
    in gray morning light
you are so beautiful waiters do not ask you to speak, they simply bring things to
    delight you,
partly because they understand beauty here is not a projection, but a possession, I
    often wonder
when you came into yours, there must have been a day you peered up at a mirror
    and there it was,
resting inside you like a flame you would not need to protect, that is another
    thing they understand,
how little one must do around it, beauty, we do not need to cup our hands, or explain
    it to itself, as if
a woman is always confused, in need of explication, desperate for someone
  to tell them
what it all means; the pink sun falling like a disk in the sky, the air blowing
  across our arms
like breath, I want to be like a park for you, dear, like a place you go
  at lunch
on days when you have time to sit by yourself and eat slowly and
  read in that lazy
way that makes your face relax, and your eyes soften, when you are
  marvelous, unobserved,
so much in your mind, your beauty is telling anyone around you all
  that is there
and I am the park, around and below and next to you, holding my breath, listening.

Why Paris Is Not the West

I have never stood
in the hollow of a tree
at Jardin du Luxembourg
and heard a train telling me,
you could be elsewhere.

Another Meal

at the park's edge a café fills
all afternoon news of the heat
wave seeping into offices
canopies roll back cutlery
clatters on smoothed white linens
steaks wheel out on platters
wine is poured near nightfall
two men stroll by ignored by
the heaving scene briefly
our gaze meets and I see
the uneaten food unrushed
evening this sea of white faces
I am not one of them as if all
my life I haven't been among
them my ease of separating
proof I am not a ghost then
the waiter asks would I care
sucks in air as he places
the spoon just so for some
dessert tonight and I play
my part well I do not say no

The Gargantuan Arm

Let us remember liberty was not popular,
seven years it took Laboulaye to convince
Bartholdi a gigantic statue was
what New York Harbor needed. Ten
years later the Frenchman
arrived in Philadelphia with her gargantuan arm.
Thirty feet high, nearly two tons of torch.
Displayed at the peak of America's backward
slide into Emancipation, it looks now
like a statue sunk in sand. So
were its finances. The same month
Jo Reed was dragged from
his cell in Nashville, Tennessee, and
hung from a suspension bridge by
an angry mob. "Hardly had Reed
been lodged in jail than the subject
of lynching him had become general
conversation," the *Memphis Daily
Appeal* reported.

Their fund-raising tour in Philadelphia
complete, Bartholdi and crew dismantled
the appendage, packed it into
crates, and loaded her on a train to New York City.
For five years the arm sat in Madison Square Park
as *Harper's* railed against Americans
having to pay for its pedestal. Raising pennies.
Coins. You could climb up inside of Liberty, it
was grand, a view. But the person taking
your ticket couldn't. People loved it. Workers
on the project back in France got married,
had children, died. Kipling came
to Paris in 1878 when Bartholdi showed
the head and was told he'd peered
through the eyes of Liberty herself. That

same month Michael Green was dragged
from his cell in Upper Marlboro, Maryland,
a noose thrown round his neck, and his
body raised fifteen feet from the ground.
Left there until the following morning.

In May of 1884, an American
businessman in Paris hosted an opulent
banquet in Bartholdi's honor, all of Parisian
society there in clothes pressed
and washed by others. Black servants
moving through the room swiftly.
Did any of the guests regard the arms
that swept over their heads to whisk
away the china and cutlery
before a new course arrived? Did they
marvel at the strength of a human-sized
arm that can carry a tray weighing thirty or
forty pounds and remain unseen?
Not spill a drop of wine or sweat.
And did any of the men waitering that
night pause for a cigarette, or
stand outside looking in at the glass
banquet hall, with its crystal
chandelier and its small-scale
model of Liberty, and know it
was not for him?

Halfway

Woken in
night's
dark basin
your hand on
my back. Fifteen
years and my
body's no longer
mine alone, it's yours,
ours. In these hours
before the street
lamps click off,
you stroll there
absentmindedly,
safe. Like
a person who
needs to walk
a familiar path
each night
before falling
asleep.

The Hand of Fate

Everyone knows if
a child is taken from
her parents, she cries,
and when they don't
return, a tiny wound
will spread across
her brain, like a bruise
on a piece of fruit,
and later, much later
when it comes time
to be chosen for
something lovely,
the selector will finger
that wound and sniff,
oh, this one's damaged,
and move on, assuming
fate put the contusion
there, rather than
a human hand.

III

The Pool

That was the terrible year.
Her imaginary friend
was playing jazz in Paris,
taking chemo; she wore
sunglasses, I arrived
exhausted, carrying
the weight of what I'd
just lost, the sun
baked down on us
cruelly, kids her age
and parents mine
on a sparkling day,
neat rows of trees,
a chance to live like
barons in a park
once a widow's palace,
gold-tipped fence posts
and all. Instead we sweated
through our clothes,
interlopers in paradise,
knowing full well
there were days
with gates closed and
visitors kicked out,
and no one but the gods
were allowed inside.

Sharing

On the bench I unwrap
a ham sandwich
ants spiders flies
caterpillars descend,
so many in a line
from my shirtsleeves
perhaps
they've been there all along.
Annoyed,
as you might be

when, emerging from an
expensive meal, you
find a beggar's hand
asking you to
reopen your wallet, how they know
to emerge when
you've more than enough to give.
All the times I've sat on this bench
with nothing to give but my presence—
how they appear
then too, not asking
but receiving me,
as do those
whose faces I've turned from
in shame,
at their generosity.

Erasures

That summer on rue du Bac
we slept for three days, then
woke one afternoon and walked
to the park, sat on a bench,
and searched the paper for a movie,
any movie, there was nothing to say,
the light too bright, the day too long,
we had to erase both. I didn't dare
touch you, there, on your chest,
where she had slept, a baby
much smaller than her pain, and you
grabbed my arm, let it go, each time
we passed someone sleeping rough,
there were so many of them, it was warm
that summer, hot even in the cinemas,
where the images flickered by and
I nearly forgot her shape on your chest
and I kept wondering if you occasionally
imagined my brother with his pack and his
dreadlocks, his searching eye
and darting walk, if you emerged like me from
the afternoon's erasure and found yourself
rising into the daylight toward a stranger,
carrying a baby turned forward like a prize,
or a man in those tatters,
who looked a little like him, as so many
Parisians did that summer, I had to assume
it was a kind of phantom of shame, if you
rushed toward them and then averted
your eyes, as if all the body didn't want
to do was rush toward pain.

Charity

In the mouth of the church
two men, three women picnic
away from the rain, a man
in rags beside them sleeping. Before
they plate sandwiches, cornichons,
fresh pears, cold meats, a piece
of bread is broken from the loaf,
wine poured into a red plastic cup
placed by his body, care taken
not to waken him.

The Waltz

Tonight in the park I was reminded of
the first waltz I attended, dancers turning
across the floor in orchestration, lights
low, the beauty of being young, trying not
to be, in our dinner jackets and dresses,
our parents' cars polished,
parked outside, still ticking in the heat,
unaware this dance was a rehearsal,
to what it wasn't clear, the movement felt
so free, endless, so much like the point
around which the entire planet orbited,
just as tonight people strolled in twos in Paris
picnicking in groups, laughing with their tongues,
lounging on chairs together—waiting for a chance dip
in light, like the lovers entwined near the empty kiosk
cooled by mists set off every ten minutes on timers,
a hiss of water meant for many, but now it's just
them in the deep green shade of the trees,
those chaperones of love's necessary discretion,
eventually it will be all of us turning and turning
out of a final cool night, we hope together, or in
twos, but it may be alone, we need each other
to face that fact, even on a night like this.

Ghost

I followed him for five laps—
the barrel-chested, twig-armed
man of eighty or so
tilting into his stride, white hair flowing,
sockless sneakers coughing across
the crushed-pebble paths.
Each lap he'd go faster,
arrow-nose piercing the air,
until light around him bent
trees unpeeled their arches,
the sky revisioned its zeppelins,
cavities carved by the war
refilled with glorious Haussmann
buildings, the undead city
around the park asking
for forgiveness, had they
known. If only they'd known
how bad it would get. Faster and faster
he runs still, until he's a mere

streak of light, Paris becoming
the undivided Jerusalem
it once was,
and he Adonis, a poet
racing to the beginning with no discernible
lack of energy.

Crow

A large black crow
beat me back to my
table at Hotel Bosnia
today. I found it poised
over my plate, wings
spread like elbows,
bent over the bread
and eggs, fruit,
things I probably
wouldn't have taken
anyway. It turned
and met my eye,
those wet, black orbs
deep and limitless,
feathers oiled like petrol-
stained water,
daring me to fathom
what it meant,
knowing my hunger
was no match
for its hunger.

Remember, Forget

I leave the city for five days,

arrow east into another
where men dropped shells
on people queuing for water and bread—
300 a day for four years
while my country did nothing. I return
and can't enter the park.
I walk its perimeter in a rage, joggers
and toddlers, lovers, legs entangled.
I begin to doubt this reality—
what is this knowledge twenty-two years
out of date, what is it worth? What
would these people do if they couldn't
sit under a tree and read the newspaper
without fear of being shot? Today in *Le Monde,*
four women crawled on their bellies
from a cellar in Mosul where they'd hid
for a month, immediately
targeted by snipers: two dead.
Everywhere new men strangling
other cities. Still, victory has been declared,
that's the headline the *Times* leads
with—and the ceasefire in Syria, declared
by the thugs grinning over their power
in Hamburg. A century from now
perhaps a memorial will stand in a park
where people can sit and take their leisure
and forget any of it ever happened, only
to be shocked again.

The Hand

I recall the trick
my father did,
disgorged his pocket,
its magical keep:
a nut, coins, a leaf,
receipt, marble, cigarette
butt. I could peek as
long as I wished
at the astonishing
yard sale he kept
in his pocket
as the girl does
in the park today,
prying open her
father's fingers.
Ah, to possess that
capacity for surprise;
June light shoots
from her eyes.
The girl's grandmother
looks on with patience,
recalling her late husband's
hands, cracked, I imagine,
like my father's, like her son's.
She knows the girl won't
ask, as I didn't ask, what
the cracks were from.

Youth

Every Sunday belfry bats of dread
flapped in the day's corners—
I raised my head at 25, at 30, then 35,
as the sun arced down, always
wretched by the coming dark.
I assumed it was the awakening
singular to humans:
one day, that day would be the last.
The gods, they hide in plain
sight in our days. Thor in
Thursday, Frigg in Friday.
Now in the Wednesday of my life,
Odin speaks as I sit
on this bench, watching a line
of schoolchildren pass,
and a more benign set of ravens
lands on my shoulders.
Those two days spent free—
every week, no workbook
or desk, just running,
drinking water, practicing home-run
swings, then the rust-warmed
burst of water from a hose, its
green tube always hot in the hand—
they were golden. I simply
did not want them to end. Two
decades and finally I see
I am free again.

Endless

Sunlight flexes
in the garden,
my screen white
with glare, I can't read
it here, tilt it this way
and that. Finally a cloud
passes and I am soaked
in cool. The porthole
opens, and there are
all the familiar things,
laid like place settings
at a meal we all think
we're hungry for,
until we sit down
to eat.

Chosen

On a lawn tanned
by sunshine I lay,
light tilting in
the sky
in gradations
of white. The sounds
of the city
far away,
like shouts in a
remembered dream.
A yellow
dog bounds into
the clearing, eyes
dark with need,
tail wagging. Alone,
its wet nose down,
then up, then down
again. Then it
is at my shin.
Reminding me what
it feels like
to be chosen, as in
you too can give.

Walks in the Dark

The woods were stark
and bluish-green, lit
by our candles, ninety
young singing boys,
walking to the lake full of
catfish and carp, holding our
fathers' hands, the white
votives dripping, the woods
darker still because of those
teardrops of light, our
fathers' hands dry and cracked
and large,
the lake its black
water absolutely waveless, and
then the candles floating out
upon it, turning its surface
liquid, showing how easy
it is to swirl darkness with a
pinprick of light, this is
what we were meant to learn,
sing to—only I remember
how the morning after I learned
the lake was a reservoir,
water we stole
from the trees that gave us
shade, and I found the dam,
holding back the hoarded
water, it was clogged
with the candles, which were
soggy and gray and not at
all like prayers.

A Moment in Time

On a windy day
I come upon a woman
crying to herself on
a bench. The park
has hidden her
in its embrace and
I must decide
how to be,
to stop or keep
walking by,
to pretend
not to see? Or
should I
flinch at her pain,
even as she,
so dedicated to
caroling her despair,
does not. How
pain does this,
makes us its
instruments.
There we were—
she weeping,
I standing, time
paused in its daily
click, and all that
was not: what
a weeper always
mourns. I could
have produced a
tissue or hugged
her. I might have
brought a bottle of
water, as if tears can

be drowned in what
they are, but I did
none of it, stilled
by that sound,
how a crane
calling over water
in the morning
is not speaking
to you.

The Missing

Every city's a ghost story,
we marble kings and kin,
but not who died building them.
Here are those who shamed for
sin, not those who died when
a church condemned.

Even today, even now there are
almost no women, but for
the Luxembourg eight or ten,
queens notable for more than
marriage to men, or for having
inspired Petrarch's pen.

Believe what elders say of ghosts,
they mean no harm, they merely want
in, remember them, they once wore
skin. Like you, and me, her and him,
us and them, and her and her and her,

and them.

Love Letter

If you were here
we'd sit outside
a while longer, wait
until the buzz of scooters
stopped   and the sky darkened,
then we'd walk home
in the tumbling light
and eat what remained
of it like fresh plums
from the windows
on Servandoni.

IV

Easement

The king instructs
the dukes,
open your gardens,
and Paris becomes

an archipelago of green.

Napoleon

moves the Medici
Fountain and the public sits so close
they can almost drink.

The Comte

de Provence, he of the
enormous library and astonishing
debts, which his grandfather

always paid, the
custody battles and
exile, he sells off a

nose of the park and

buys a new horse.

The new king is not
a king but he makes

adjustments

like the rest.
He sends his plain-
clothed men

to the park to sweep
out refugees with
their swinging batons.

What if we have this
wrong, maybe

what is tough is history,
and what is progress
is greed. And what
needs adjustment
lives outside the park,
not in?

Autumn

Out of a cinema's
cool blue cave
into the brassy fall
light, sun arcing
toward building tops.
Hard to see how
necrotic film is
until you compare
it to Paris at three p.m.
in October,
cafés on the park
heaving, plane
trees in
fragrant decline,
the dry papery
hands of elderly
men gripped tight
to their wives.
They're no longer
too proud for
help, the
battles of spring
long behind them.

Song of the Songs

I wish we were living
a story of desire, but
I don't feel Odysseus
beating out his tale
of longing at the oars
as we row toward this
war. I don't sense
a heart burning, this is
just vengeance, not
even tragic because
the fire that will rain
down does not say,
take my son and I
will scorch this earth—
some of us
could appreciate an
aria of pain. A mouth
shaped to a horn
playing one terrible
note. But we don't even
get that sound, it is drowned
by the other, the one
heard every day
now, it says more,
I can do anything, watch
me engulf the world,
oh Lord, I am greater
than even you.

On Memory & Desire

How many recall
the park
as skin

unpuckering

on their
knees, an
afterimage

of gravel,
desire's tarry
chark.

Names

They say it is like being
stabbed by a thousand tiny
knives, your skin
one long throat, coated
in acid. I suppose that
means survivors
have said so. Witnesses
observe that
when the outer
layer of dermis cracks,
fat seeps out and feeds
the flames. Then you can
burn for hours. In the Middle Ages,
people tied to the stake often died of
smoke inhalation. Perhaps
Mohamed Bouazizi hadn't
done his research,
didn't know how very unpleasant
it would be. Or perhaps it
is just as inconceivable to
imagine what
his life had been like
since he was a child.
His produce taken,
pissed on, his pockets
disgorged, the same
two cops strolling
by day after day,
their jackal smiles
and busy hands,
how low do you need to be
to rob a man selling produce
from a wagon?
They took it all, everything, some-

times giving his weighing
scales back,
sometimes asking for more.
Maybe they made him
suck their dicks
or eat their shit,
promise his sister,
while they spat on him.
Day after day year after
each year deeper
in hock to pay
for a day always
hungrier than his customers,
the mustaches always
returning. I will
do it, he said
when he made a complaint,
I will light myself on fire
if you don't give me my
scales back. Three witnesses
heard him say this before
the court, which refused to hear
his case. Then he used the
last of his money, bought
a can of gasoline, stood in
the street turning his body to
one long wick
and asked, how do you expect
me to live? What happened next
was superior to dying a little
every day. The president
of Tunisia visited Bouazizi
in hospital shortly before
he died. Promised his family

to fly their dying son to Paris
for first-class treatment. Bouazizi
declined with his death. There
are no statues to him yet,
just a movement. The Arab
Spring, they called it, like
a cool breeze.

The Abacus

We sit steps from the east gate, watching guards direct
visitors from the park. His bald head now a torch. Will I
follow him on this path? Each gulp of wine blows on the
flames that flicker around us. I am not the first he has led
here, I know. Maybe it is every night, or once a week. This
rocky cave we must duck into in plain sight. The gust of
cold air. His turning back, saying, *Let us swallow this fire,
it is why they need us.* Station to station we walk and squint
into each blaze. He lingers before the most hideous inferno.
At last we reach the innermost black. *Have you ever told a
woman her child is dead, John?* I think he asked this, but
maybe the collapsing day had just sparked on stone. The
interior is like night, moonlit, blue-lit. So quiet as if there
has been only us. He wants me to watch him do the old
addition. We sit upon the floor of the world. Each bead
clicks against the next, making a chain as he measures them
for me in the dark. The beads have been painted different
colors. We are the only ones here. *I am not like them,* he
says, upon finishing, telling me his inconceivable score. I
can swallow all this fire, his face a skeleton, his eyes like
candelabra, his mouth a reburn so black I can't see its edges,
and at night, it lights nothing, not even the path back.

Between

I am swimming
in time again. A warm
tide carries me to sea
and I tread for hours,
my legs
weary with delirium,
and on other
days a cold swift
current glides beneath me and
I brace myself. How
to be both, this
watchful, moving
thing, tipped up
to the light, receiving
as if nothing ever
sank of its ability
to float.

Choice

Everything's on sale,
shoes, handbags,
wineglasses, soap.
Pianos, rugs, underwear.
Soldes Soldes Soldes!
I see the word so much
it ceases to mean
anything. I decide
today it should mean
love. *Love Love Love!*
All day a classic-car rally
parades Saint-Germain-des-
Prés. Key-lime
Corvettes, Mustangs
with bright-red window
dice, rattletrap VWs.
There's even a
Citroën 508 you can
take a twirl in with a
real-life French grandmother
sitting in the backseat
muttering about the
weather. After nightfall
I walk home
on a darkened street,
the only light
an *atelier*
d'architecture. Inside
a woman bends into
a cone of light. I decide
she's God, designing
the world where we
don't have to choose
optimism.

Hands

Just twice, in forty-three years,
have I felt one upon me. First,
outside a Seventh Avenue bar. It took
some time to find the arm and torso
and face to which it belonged,
a long moonish one turned to the side
as if embarrassed

by its hand's behavior. I cannot help it,
the face said. Then,
a decade before, dancing in a club
in San Francisco, a furious
scrabbling, again, unattached,
as if, unabated, hands would
all be on the lam, scrambling
across trousers and skirts,

chased by embarrassed owners
seeking pity for
their plight. Just twice
and I have walked home
late at night, I have
forgotten how I arrived there,
I have taken off my clothes
for money, I have erased

so many hours, and just twice have
I found such hands, as if
for forty-three years
the world has been one large,
well-lit park, a night watchman
spinning his nightstick
chasing them away, saying,
Carry on, carry on.

Stitch

They wore white breasts, like scarves, their hundred heads
turned to us from the blue wood, making the deer's eyes
seem like parts of one large invisible body only gradually
showing itself in stripes of winter, she talking as they strode
ahead in car coats and Wellingtons, striding across the
grounds talking of how she allowed her husband to pay but
then paid his bills, *He likes to feel like a man,* the two of us
behind, the men, talking of her, as usual, while I wanted to
say, *Don't you see that hillside, that moving hillside right there?*
But it was backdrop, part of the perpetual park in which
they lived, part of the design, here is nature, here are some
new guests, the game recast, before new eyes or ears, in
this season or that and the eyes, they watched in hundreds,
wanting to know, were we good, did we mean well, and on
that day I could not speak my answer.

The Folded Wing

The lone duck in
Medici Fountain
slips her beak
beneath a wing
and falls asleep.
Drifting like a
hat tossed into
a green pond.
How good it feels
to be one's own
comfort, to discover
all the warmth we
need buried in
our bodies. Yes

we bleed, we are
broken, we get
just one body, yet
there it lies most of
the time, calling
to us, saying, rest here,
lie down in me, I
am more than less
than you, even in a
world that treats
us as two.

Light

I'd been in the flat six weeks
before I learned to raise the blinds.
Falling asleep to reddish light,
waking to the sounds of traffic.
I'd emerge from its murky cave
taking as truth that mornings
hung as low-lit lanterns,
I would always be behind
things, never with them,
the world always to be
approached, slowly, from a
distance, before it could be
entered, like an illuminated
party for which I was late,
and knew no one. All I'd
needed to do was tie a small
string around a metal star,
and the sun began to touch
my forehead gently at
first light, as my grandmother
did many years ago when
I visited and each day
arrived like a gift, something
miraculous and strange
she had given me.

Dinner at the End of the World

Café tables
once faced
the boulevard
so diners could
take in the
promenade;
now it seems
they're turned
that way so we
will spot the
faces of beggars
coming and know
when to look down.

Marriage

A man and a woman joined
by newspaper pages
culture to politics
sit so still I'm not sure
whether they're there
at all. She breathes
turns a ruffled folio
and like a dancer moving
around a partner he folds
a great page in two
and peers up in expectation
of what he needs to know.

An hour passes—they do this
five times. Not once
do they pivot to each other.
Not once do they break
the spell. Later, as they return
home, she'll turn to him
and report the astonishing events
that took place in the park
that day and he'll listen

with interest and alarm,
then ask what it is they ought to eat
that night—and a new dance

they've practiced so often it happens
as if by nature, by fate, by fortune,
will begin anew.

Paris at Night

We school into the roke
rattle-slat windows
chuffing air—
hip to bone through
stark white tunnels
a river aspiring to mist,
then up and up
onto rain-dark streets,
lights glorying the night,
wine and cheeses,
brumal feasts for a sundered
day, sirens
caroling in the distance.

Acknowledgments

The following poems appeared in the following publications. I am grateful for their editors.

Common: "Modern Gods," "Translation in Paris"

Michigan Quarterly Review: "Seeing Things"

Narrative: "Charity," "The City Without," "Remember, Forget," "Sharing"

New England Review: "Teacher"

Orion: "Birds"

A Public Space: "In a Bucharest Journal"

Virginia Quarterly Review: "The Gargantuan Arm," "Song of the Songs," "Weight"

Zyzzyva: "Stitch"

About the Author

John Freeman is the editor of *Freeman's*, a literary biannual, and author of the poetry collections *Maps* and *The Park*, as well as three books of nonfiction, *Dictionary of the Undoing*, *The Tyranny of E-mail*, and *How to Read a Novelist*. He has also edited three anthologies of writing on inequality, including *Tales of Two Americas* and *Tales of Two Planets*, a new book about global inequality and climate change. The former editor of *Granta*, he lives in New York, where he is writer-in-residence at New York University. The executive editor at *LitHub*, he has published poems in *Zyzzyva*, *The New Yorker*, *The Paris Review*, and *The Nation*. His work has been translated into more than twenty languages.

Poetry is vital to language and living. Since 1972, Copper Canyon Press has published extraordinary poetry from around the world to engage the imaginations and intellects of readers, writers, booksellers, librarians, teachers, students, and donors.

WE ARE GRATEFUL FOR THE MAJOR SUPPORT PROVIDED BY:

THE PAUL G. ALLEN
FAMILY FOUNDATION

Anonymous

Jill Baker and Jeffrey Bishop

Anne and Geoffrey Barker

Donna and Matthew Bellew

Diana Broze

John R. Cahill

The Beatrice R. and Joseph A. Coleman Foundation Inc.

The Currie Family Fund

Laurie and Oskar Eustis

Saramel and Austin Evans

Mimi Gardner Gates

Gull Industries Inc. on behalf of William True

The Trust of Warren A. Gummow

Carolyn and Robert Hedin

Phil Kovacevich and Eric Wechsler

Lakeside Industries Inc.

on behalf of Jeanne Marie Lee

Maureen Lee and Mark Busto

Peter Lewis

TO LEARN MORE ABOUT UNDERWRITING
COPPER CANYON PRESS TITLES,
PLEASE CALL 360-385-4925 EXT. 103

WE ARE GRATEFUL FOR THE MAJOR SUPPORT PROVIDED BY:

Ellie Mathews and Carl Youngmann as The North Press

Larry Mawby

Hank Meijer

Jack Nicholson

Petunia Charitable Fund and adviser Elizabeth Hebert

Gay Phinny

Suzie Rapp and Mark Hamilton

Adam and Lynn Rauch

Emily and Dan Raymond

Jill and Bill Ruckelshaus

Cynthia Sears

Kim and Jeff Seely

Dan Waggoner

Randy and Joanie Woods

Barbara and Charles Wright

Caleb Young as C. Young Creative

The dedicated interns and faithful volunteers
of Copper Canyon Press

The Chinese character for poetry is made up of two parts:
"word" and "temple."
It also serves as pressmark for Copper Canyon Press.

This book is set in Adobe Garamond.
Design by Katy Homans.
Printed on archival-quality paper.

CPSIA information can be obtained
at www.ICGtesting.com
Printed in the USA
LVHW010121170120
643905LV00004B/6